BUSTA RHYME

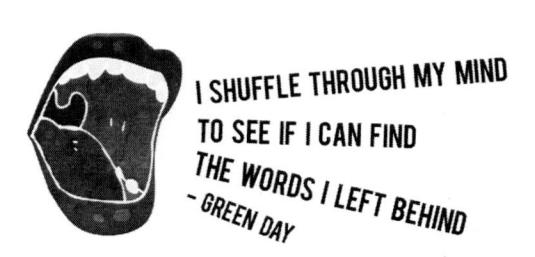

> I SHUFFLE THROUGH MY MIND TO SEE IF I CAN FIND THE WORDS I LEFT BEHIND
> – GREEN DAY

THE SOUTH WEST

Edited By Allie Jones

First published in Great Britain in 2017 by:

YoungWriters
Est. 1991

Young Writers
Coltsfoot Drive
Peterborough
PE2 9BF
Telephone: 01733 890066
Website: www.youngwriters.co.uk

All Rights Reserved
Book Design by Spencer Hart
© Copyright Contributors 2017
SB ISBN 978-1-78820-975-5
Printed and bound in the UK by BookPrintingUK
Website: www.bookprintinguk.com
YB0315NZ

FOREWORD

Welcome Reader,

For Young Writers' competition, *Busta Rhyme*, we asked secondary school pupils to take inspiration from the world around them, whether from the news, their own lives or even songs, and then write a poem on any subject of their choice. They rose to the challenge magnificently, with young writers up and down the country displaying their poetic talent.

Poems were selected for publication based on style, expression, imagination and technical skill. The result is this entertaining collection full of diverse and imaginative poetry which covers a variety of topics - from football dreams and seasonal descriptions, to more serious subjects such as political strife, bullying, racism and war. Using poetry as their tool, the young writers have taken this opportunity to express their thoughts and feelings through verse. This anthology is also a delightful keepsake to look back on in years to come.

Here at Young Writers, our aim is to encourage creativity in the next generation and to inspire a love of the written word, so it was great to receive such an amazing response, and some absolutely fantastic poems. I'd like to congratulate all the young poets in this anthology, I hope this inspires them to continue with their creative writing journey.

Allie Jones

CONTENTS

Barnwood Park Arts College, Gloucester

Daisy-May Chambers (16)	1
Michelle Nicholas (12)	2
Bethany Jane Gelder (14)	5
Safa Siddiq (13)	6
Husnaa Patel (13)	7
Megan Ractliffe (13)	8

Honiton Community College, Honiton

Oshi Welch (13)	10
Mara Gaches (13)	13
Caitlin Jamie Fowler (14)	14
Emily Burroughs (13)	16
Sammy Paveley (13)	19
Marnie Osborne (13)	20
Kiera Bonetta (14)	22
Jack Hawker (14)	24
Elliott Green (12)	26
Laura-Beth Outram (14)	28
Nathan Turner (12)	29
Elliot Leadbeater (11)	30
Sam Steel (14)	31
Mason Druin Doble (11)	32
Louisa Jones (13)	33
Zac Lancaster (11)	34
Emily Rose Ashby (11)	35
Kieran Laker (13)	36
Reese Cottington (11)	37
Florence Gray (11)	38
Cherry Dale (12)	39
Sophie Louise Phillips (12)	40
Daniel Loosemore (14)	41

Jamie Wallis (11)	42
Michelle O'Malley (11)	43
Zara Maynard (12)	44
Aaliyah Anna Freeman (11)	45
Ruby Drew (11)	46
Dylan Williams (12)	47
Caleb Freemantle (14)	48
Jacob Rose (11)	49
Thomas Cameron Elliott (11)	50

Kingsley School, Bideford

Reuben Cobb (14)	51
Kitty Lavelle (14)	52
Tolly Land (13)	54
Amy Macwilliam (13)	55
Rupert George (12)	56
Hugo Wells (11)	57
Aaron Smyth (12)	58
Ben Hansen (12)	59
Harry Lucas (12)	60
Poppy Goaman (12)	61

Rednock School, Dursley

Zoë Clutterbuck (12)	62
Owen Dennis Dyas Jones (12)	64
Natasha Trinder (13)	66
Alice Smith (12)	67
Charlotte Morse (12)	68
Cara Pickard (12)	69
Isabella Delrosa (12)	70
Hollie Jean Walton (12)	71
Scarlett Maule (12)	72
Nathan Curry (11)	73
Alanah Williams (12)	74

Charlotte Tuckwell (13)	76
Harrison Page (11)	77
Millie Young (12)	78
Holly Morris (12)	79
Amy Winfield (13)	80
Mia Richardson (11)	81
Charlie Utting (11)	82
Lizzy Dunn (11)	83
James Moir (11)	84
Lauren Whittaker (12)	85
Courtney Phillips (11)	86

Saltash.Net Community School, Saltash

Kieran Playne (12)	87
Mia Kenworthy (12)	88
Daniel Collins (14)	89
Ryan Coulson (14)	90
Jack Hawes (11)	92
Thomas Kinver (14)	93
Megan Slocombe (15)	94
Jess Burgess (11)	95
Laura Hackworthy (12)	96
Elliot Jordan (14)	97
Thomas Perry (15)	98
Connor Laker (13)	99
Erin Jordan (12)	100
Oscar Price (16)	101
Saffron Paice (15)	102
Matthew Pean (13)	103
Daisy Lane (12)	104

Sidcot School, Winscombe

Evie Ward (12)	105
Hannah Peters (14)	106
Maggie Hammond (13)	108
Elsa Kerstin Cardale (11)	110
Lucy Zeeman (13)	112
Ruby Cogan (13)	114
Sarah Carr (14)	115
James Barber (14)	116
Luca Cuckson (11)	118

Mackensie Jones (12)	120
Hannah Fairley (14)	121
Isabella Hoddell (12)	122
Jacob Perry (14)	124
Jim Mitchell (14)	125
William Sandiford (12)	126
Claudia Jarman (11)	127
Amelia Carveth (14)	128

St Peter's CE (A) School, Exeter

Abby Middlebrooke (14)	129
Alice Dean (14)	130
Jemeya Molindo (14)	133
Hannah Quinn (15)	134
Samuel L Vile (14)	136
Jessica Yates (15)	138
Mimi Mugford (15)	140
Joseph McLaughlin (15)	141
Maddie Arnold (15)	142
Izzie Auty-Dawe (15)	144
Eleanor Olivia Kerr (15)	145
Freya Fanson (15)	146
Josh Nicholas (15)	147
Isobel Pinsky (15)	148
Asher Condon-Jones (15)	150
Ellen Billingsley (13)	151
Anna Vukusic (15)	152
Tristan Bentall (15)	153
Rufus Stanier (14)	154

Stoke Damerel Community College, Plymouth

Bracken Kerr (12)	155
Jasmine Wilkins (12)	156
Bethany Hawkey (12)	158
Khloe Lyndon (13)	159
Alexandra Maticiuc (12)	160
Lucy Chugg (11)	161
Sam Rickard (12)	162
Alana Hallybone (12)	163
Joe Maddick (14)	164
Lauren Ann Martin (11)	165

Katelyn Bell (12)	166
Bradley Burgess (13)	167
Klaudia Zawadzka (11)	168
Cody Coombe (11)	169

The Kings Of Wessex Academy, Cheddar

Thea Scott	170

The Park Community School, Barnstaple

Dylan Skinner (12)	172
Lily Wilson (12)	173
Phoebe Clarke (11)	174
Lexus Jayne Dryden (12)	175
Lucy Camp (12)	176
Madison Fishleigh (11)	177
Poppy Tallin (11)	178
Lucie May Sandwell (11)	179
Ben Robinson (11)	180
Rosie Anderson-Retter (12)	181

THE POEMS

Gun

A gun to my head.
My finger on the trigger.
I can put the gun down for it to be picked back up by them
Either I pull the trigger or they do.
I am a hostage to my own hands
I am a hostage to them
Hands over my mouth aren't just mine
They constrict me; I can't shout for help, I can't stop them
They sit whispering pestilent words in my ear.
They pace the room repeating their lines.
There are many of them.
Uncountable.
Some characters stand out more.
They are the unforgettable ones.
They are the ones that pull the trigger.
Bang!
But there was no gun.
They are still there but they aren't human.
They are my mental illnesses.
They are living in my head rent free.
They rip me up and break my stitches.
They control my every move.
I am their puppet.
I can break free but the strings are like chains.
Heavy.

Daisy-May Chambers (16)
Barnwood Park Arts College, Gloucester

The Vision Of A Slave

Five years a slave
Ten years a slave
It doubles and doubles
I need to be saved

Locked in a safe
Desperate for air
The gas came so suddenly
My last breath in fear

Five years a slave
Ten years a slave
It doubles and doubles
I need to be saved

Pleading to go home
While being whipped on my back
The things I feel and see
It's my life, but there's much I lack

Five years a slave
Ten years a slave
It doubles and doubles
I need to be saved

Just a lad
Who wants to be cool
Yet instead of playing
I work like a mule

Five years a slave
Ten years a slave
It doubles and doubles
I need to be saved

The minute he locked the door
There was nowhere to turn
The uncomfortable pain I endured
Felt like an unending burn

Five years a slave
Ten years a slave
It doubles and doubles
I need to be saved

Can't escape this life
Of fame, fortune and doom
Moth to the mic, eyes to the light
Yet not singing to my own tune

Five years a slave
Ten years a slave
It doubles and doubles
I need to be saved

Stop with the torture
Your words are cutting deep
Going through the night
With hardly any sleep

Five years a slave
Ten years a slave
One day I hope
To no longer be caged.

Michelle Nicholas (12)
Barnwood Park Arts College, Gloucester

We've Destroyed Our Only Earth

We've polluted the air and contaminated oceans,
Cut down billions of trees,
Our source of oxygen, the thing we need to breathe.
We've driven innocent animals to extinction,
Taking away your chances to ever meet them,
We say that race is no longer a problem,
Nor sexism, religion or who you love,
But we still start wars and kill others,
Just because they are different.
We don't do anything to help people,
Instead just make excuses,
We stereotype everyone:
'Muslims are terrorists', 'black people are criminals'.
We don't help those in need,
Leaving them without education, clean water or vital medicines,
Too busy making new machines and
Upgrading our technology because
We're all full of greed.
We've caused destruction to everyone and everything,
We've destroyed our only earth...

Bethany Jane Gelder (14)
Barnwood Park Arts College, Gloucester

Dementia

Remember the time you built sandcastles with me,
even though they kept washing away? No?

Remember that time when everyone turned their back on me
and you stood there with the door wide open? No?

I do. I remember everything. Every memory is engraved in the depths of my heart,
every word echoes in my brain. Every gesture is reflected in my being.

Your memories are firmly placed on the tip of my tongue,
ready to lighten up the darkest rooms.

I desperately attempt to rekindle your thoughts.
I'm fighting with the inevitable even though
it's breaking my own heart.

As your thoughts disappear, mine question my mental stability.

As you forget, I desperately remember.

I remember, I will remember for you.

Safa Siddiq (13)
Barnwood Park Arts College, Gloucester

Equality Matters, Right?

Equality matters, right?
Then what happened to those,
those before us,
who fought for equality.
Martin Luther King,
the suffragettes,
or even Rosa Parks?

Think about how others feel,
to be different,
or do the feelings of those,
who are different not matter?
We all want peace but,
there's no peace without
equality.

What are we teaching the
next generation?
We are teaching them to
love with hate and to
hate with love.
One day we are all going to
wish to go back to
the peaceful world we never were.

Husnaa Patel (13)
Barnwood Park Arts College, Gloucester

Homework

We need free time
To live and enjoy
To have fun and play
Relax and unwind

They have our days
We should have our nights
It's like a maze
And now we're lost in a maze

If it's not done
Whatever the reason
We will get a series of detentions
No matter the reason

Some may enjoy it
Others may not
We all have a variety of abilities
Challenging for some, easy for others

We find it unfair
Kid you not
We know why it's there
But that's not enough

We want to do well
But not give up our free time
We need time to think
Relax and unwind!

Megan Ractliffe (13)
Barnwood Park Arts College, Gloucester

Labels And Equality

What is discrimination for?
All it creates is even more war.
Whether it's disability, race or religion,
No one should face it without good rhyme or reason
Everyone is different and that's not treason
Labels should be banned not used as categorisation
After all, we are each to our own
We are human.

Race shows love and diversity in all that live
It's not there to create hate and cruelty
Just because someone has a different ethnicity or colour,
Doesn't mean they are unsatisfactory or second best,
In fact, the truth is the opposite like everyone else
Loyal, loving and kind.
If all else fails,
They are human.

The same goes for religion,
If someone thinks a certain way that is not harmful
to humanity, let them be.
War is only the result of prejudice and inequality
Without religion the world would be lonely
and not turn the way it does today.
Religion is considerate, intelligent and generous,
Not one is a malicious, destructive terrorist

Those who commit crimes are not religious
Only using it as a label to brand
others with a bad name for no reason
other than disrespect
After all,
They are human.

The labels that are given to those with disability,
Only evoke sadness and pity
Just looking 'normal'
doesn't bring normality.
Physical struggles don't mean intellectual difficulty,
Those who live with disability are only striving
For life like you and me.
In fact, they are stronger than we will ever be.
Casting aspersions and blanket statements
Doesn't bring self-respect, just words that are derogatory
Living with a disability shows strength and tenacity
Not helplessness and instability.
After all,
They are human.

Equality will never be perfect,
But for the moment it can be more in effect
Lives will be lived,
Beliefs will be believed
And problems will be solved

Labels should be banned, not used as categorisation
After all we are each to our own,
We are human.

Oshi Welch (13)
Honiton Community College, Honiton

Music

Music, the beat and the rhythm that courses through your veins
The only medicine that soothes the soul and heals the heart.
The only thing that actually understands you in every way possible,
That listens, that helps, that loves you in your darkest hour.
For when you feel alone and confused, and the times get rough
When no one understands, and you don't feel tough.
Music will be there,
When you're alone on the street and someone catcalls you
When you can't find your way and no one will help you
When you're scared and afraid and there's no light to guide you
Music will show you the way
The emotions that music portrays
You could feel sadness, anger, happiness, confusion, empathy, all in one second of music.
You could feel like you were in a different world, another lifetime.
Music is made so you feel the emotions that you thought you lost.
Music is made so you can feel the happiness you've been lacking
Music is made, and enjoyed by the people of the world who want to share their emotions with you and only you.
Music, the beat and the rhythm that courses through your veins.

Mara Gaches (13)
Honiton Community College, Honiton

Boys Will Be Boys And Girls Are Their Toys

When we were young,
We were told that if boys picked on us, they liked us.
So we stayed silent and didn't cause a fuss,
While the boys poked, prodded and pulled on our pigtails.
We had enough, so just once did we yell,
Only to be told that boys will be boys
And girls are only thought of as their toys.
Just pretty dolls to treat as they wish
They chase us with lips puckered and we hope they miss.

We all grew older and blossomed into womanhood,
While boys still acted as boys supposedly should.
We had been taught to look good for our male peers
Giving them their chances to catcall and leer.
Yes we were never told to look good for our own peace of mind
Only that if we didn't look pleasing then
The boys were allowed to be unkind.

We base our opinions on the eyes of men and their views,
Even after they've cornered us in the nightclub loos.
He lurches towards you with alcohol on his breath
and sex on his mind
You realise you really don't have much time
You can't run away in your heels too high
The music is too loud, they can't hear you cry!

His hands grope forwards and take you by the arms
Your mind is screaming with warnings and alarms
He moves forwards faster and your dignity drops lower
And suddenly time seems to move much slower.

Every girl has pictured her bright white knight on a noble steed,
But they are just lies which boys use as a lead
To pull a young vulnerable girl
And watch their sick fantasies unfurl.
So we go home once its over
Bowing our head down even lower
And keeping our mouths shut tightly
Not letting on, not even slightly!
Because girls have been taught that boys will be boys
And we are only here as their pretty toys
Apparently.
But we are people and we deserve respect!
We are not your playthings!
We dress the way we do to let our personalities sing!
We are not here to be criticised
And we will no longer fall for those lies
We are girls
You are boys
And we will no longer be your toys!

Caitlin Jamie Fowler (14)
Honiton Community College, Honiton

Bullying Hurts

Bullying hurts,
It starts with one word, one word you blurt
'Fat', 'Loser', 'Ugly', these are the words they hear
Did you know, you're their biggest fear?

Every day they wake up with regret,
Trying hard to forget
It's not just the physical abuse
Words shoot daggers too.

After a while enough is enough
Sick of being brave, of being tough
They try to stand up but are pulled back down,
Why do you have to turn their smile into a frown?

Your words always offend
They can't be glued back together again
Standing, crowding, imposing.

Someone breaks the circle and offers them a hand
They learn they can now stand.
That smile is no longer fake
They now don't need to ache.

All they needed was a friend
Someone to be with when it all came again.
They are free,
All your insults barely sting, see.

Now I'll tell you something.

You are a bully,
The bully is not wanted unless to leave see,
Your work here is done,
Not that it ever should have started
Now don't you feel a bit broken-hearted?

Bullying gave you power,
Now that's gone all sour,
Now you wonder, *what if?*
What if they didn't get so strong
Would they have crumbled all along?

You wonder what could have been,
Could that knife have touched their skin
You might have pushed them over the edge
They might have been found dead behind a hedge.

You don't know what could have been done
And you thought it was just for fun.
You think they are weak,
But they are stronger than you
All the things you put them through
Just think, all of those black eyes.

So go away bully, say your goodbyes
But before you go,
Remember one thing,
The memory of a bully never dies.

And you are a bully.

Emily Burroughs (13)
Honiton Community College, Honiton

Why I Love Watford FC

FA Cup in 1984, the team I just adore, that's why I have everything in the store,
Dedication to Graham Taylor, he has his own stand
That's why Elton John supports the best team in the land
Second in Division 1 in the 1980s
That was before the days of stupid transfer fees
Deeney is the best, with pride he wears the crest
When we beat Man United, all our fans were enlightened
Okaka scored a double, causing Everton trouble
Ighalo's number 24 but this season he's struggled to score.

Players don't get weighed down by fame,
Even if they're a big name
Pereyra dances with his rapid feet
Watching him is a guaranteed treat
I support Watford, Watford is my team
Playing for Watford would be my dream
They may not have millions of pounds,
But the fans chanting is one of the best sounds
We always keep going, keep up the fight
Whether we play at Stamford Bridge or the Stadium of Light.

Sammy Paveley (13)
Honiton Community College, Honiton

Would You?

The official definition of an animal is:

A living creature, having sensation and power of voluntary motion
Let's explore the accuracy of this.

'A living creature'
Living: existence
Their hearts beat, therefore they exist
They live, they are real.

'Living sensation'
All animals have these five senses

1 Touch, petting of hitting them can evoke this sense
2 Taste, they can taste the treats that we lovingly lavish them with
3 Sight, they see all emotions
4 Smell, dogs in particular have the best sense of smell - even better than ours
5 Hearing, they respond with loyalty when you bark their names

Some animals have even evolved new senses
Echo location for example.

'Power of voluntary motion'
Now, this one flummoxed me
Do they offer to sacrifice their life for a perfume?
Are they deformed and tortured out of their own free will?

No
Why would you let yourself become a source of experimentation
For something that is of no use to you?
Millions of innocent animals are forced onto tables every year,
Injected with a substance that has the potential to kill them or worse
Maim them!

Do you know what happens when they are useless,
Too mangled to be of any use?
They are tossed out like trash.

Oblivious to the goings on around them
Suddenly pierced with a needle
Drowning in pain, fear and bewilderment
No means of communication their distress

So next time you use an animal-tested product
or receive an injection
Just remember, an animal has been sacrificed for something
You could live without
That item will be discarded, just like them
That body wash is equivalent to three mice lives
Gone

So, do you think that the definition of animal is accurate?

Marnie Osborne (13)
Honiton Community College, Honiton

This Is A Stereotype

A stereotype -
Fixed images or ideas,
Types of people or a thing,
Typically regarded as a disgrace to society.
Three dimensional, fake perceptions,
Associations widely held by many,
Why should these people be treated so differently?

Homelessness -
Worthless people?
They're genuine people like you and me,
Just slightly more unfortunate,
All they did was pull life's short straw,
But ended up coming out stronger than before.

LGBT Community -
Are all gay men feminine?
Are all transgenders fake?
Sexual orientation doesn't determine one's personality,
Nor does it change what they like or their style.
Gender is not defined by a skirt,
Nor should it change your love for the people around you.

Racism -
Associating black people with evil?
People should not be labelled to racial traits,
They are not a colour,
And what is a colour to determine who we are?

A stereotype -
Fixed images or ideas,
Widely held and oversimplified.
Don't judge the homeless until you know their story,
These people are stronger than you and I will ever be.
If the LGBT Community owe an explanation,
Why don't we owe one for our straightness?
Black people should be judged by their personality and charm,
Not by the shade of their skin.

We live in a judgemental, cliché world where things are too easily stereotyped.
These days we are more comfortable seeing two men holding guns than two men holding hands!
No person should be discriminated against for fake perceptions.
Never judge anyone by their current state until you know what they battled through to get there.
And, most importantly,
Treat these people with the respect they deserve.
Nothing has and nothing ever will fit the stereotypical label it has been stuck to.

Kiera Bonetta (14)
Honiton Community College, Honiton

Chelsea FC

Chelsea FC, Chelsea are my pride
And I support them with such great pride.
If you love football there's a team you choose
I will follow Chelsea even when they lose.
People bleed red, but I bleed blue,
Chelsea, Chelsea, Chelsea is all that I do.
The fans will fly, the blue flag high
All the way up to the sky,
Stamford Bridge is where we play
The fans travel to watch us play away.
Eden Hazard nets again,
This time I believe we will score ten.
John Terry and David Luiz
Help us with their defending expertise,
Seven FA Cups and four Premier Leagues,
We have a great play style that keeps all intrigued.
But now this year we're five points clear
And the end of the Premier League is near,
I have seen a lot of Chelsea's games
And even been on a tour
And as a Chelsea fan I crave more and more
At Stamford Bridge you can hear the fans chanting
Our team is so great we think we are outstanding.
Glory hunters is what they call us
Even when we finish tenth
Our fans still stick by us with trust

N'golo Kanté and Antonio Conte
Are certainly no castaways,
Blue is the colour and football is the game
We're all together and winning is our game,
So cheer us on through the sun and rain
Because Chelsea is our name.

Jack Hawker (14)
Honiton Community College, Honiton

Cyber

Has the convenience of technology
Inoculated us from reality?
Do androids dream of electric sheep?
I pray the code my soul to keep
Does your universe live with 4G
Or megapixel infinity?
Which memory lies within
The one that was
Or the one that's been,
Or how much gig, how much ram?
Which reality is true?
Cyber me
Or cyber you?
Cyber bully
Cyber crime?
Cyber hate
Cyber time?
Cyber boxer
Or cyber brief?
Who is the real identity thief?
Cyber pleasure
Cyber pain
Hours spent glaring into the screen
Choosing an alternate username.
Status updates and trending tweets
Fill your mind and rob your sleep.

Clever hashtags and Instagram
Will shape your image and gain more friends.
Is the you you've shaped in cyberspace
The same you I'd see face-to-face?
We hide behind our computer screens
A criticise with brutal ease.
Virtual reality.

Elliott Green (12)
Honiton Community College, Honiton

Football Is Really Fun

F ootball is really fun
O h I'm not done
O n top of the fun
T he sport is enjoyable
B ut can be competitive
A s it is like a race to first place
L ots of laughs, lessons and perseverance to
L earn to never give up

I t is not just about kicking a ball and to fall but to
S upport one another and to work as a team

R unning is active
E asy to say the fact is, it is tiring after a while
A great team is Manchester United who
L ose quite a few yet they win too
L osing is not so bad although
Y ou do get mad

F inishing a smashing goal could lead to a win
U p and up the table you go
N umber one in the table will get people to cheer rather than say no.

Football is really fun.

Laura-Beth Outram (14)
Honiton Community College, Honiton

The Monkey

Monkey, monkey in the tree
Oh, so very far from me,
Do you see me on the ground
As you're swinging all around?

How dearly I would love to be
A monkey sat up in a tree,
How I'd love to be like you
I wonder if you watch me too?

Are you lonely in that tree
Or do you have a family?
Are your friends as nice as mine?
Tell me how you spend your time.

Monkey, monkey in the sky
Why do you sit there? Why oh why?
If you could talk, what would you say?
Oh, why do you sit there all day?

Do you ever look down on me?
All lonely, sat up in that tree
Do you watch me down below?
If you could speak, would you say hello?

Monkey, monkey in the tree
Who I wish I could be
As I quietly pass by,
I nod my head to say goodbye.

Nathan Turner (12)
Honiton Community College, Honiton

The Sailor's Shanty

There once was a sailor who lived on the sea
Hi-ho, hi-ho, hi-ho Mary go
There once was a sailor who fished happily
Hi-ho, hi-ho, hi-ho Mary go
But then a huge kraken appears from the sea
Oh no, oh no, oh no Mary go
It was feeling very hungry indeed
Oh no, oh no, oh no Mary go
It soon saw the sailor and felt more hungry
Uh-oh, uh-oh, uh-oh Mary go
The beast soon got near and got ready to kill
Uh-oh, uh-oh, uh-oh Mary go
The sailor saw the beast and gave it a pill
Hi-ho, hi-ho, hi-ho Mary go
The kraken felt better and thanked the sailor
Oh yay, oh yay, oh yay, hip hooray
The sailor went home with the catch of the day
Oh yay, oh yay, oh yay, hip hooray
The ocean was now free from the kraken
The end, the end, the end, yay, hooray!

Elliot Leadbeater (11)
Honiton Community College, Honiton

For The Love Of The Game

Football. The game loved by millions.
Young kids watching Ronaldo dance through defences like a knife through butter;
Watching Manuel Neuer make a save from a shot arrowing into the top corner.
A dream is born,
And will never die.

We do it for the last-minute thrills,
For those nail-biting moments
We do it for those bum-on-the-edge-of-the-sofa moments
The fists clenched, sweaty and sticky foreheads
We do it for the love of the game.

We do it for those cup-winning goals,
The injury time winner causing the fans to descend into mayhem
We do it to see the crowd erupt like a volcano, chanting the scorer's name
We do it for the hugs of celebration,
The fists-punching-the-air moments.
We do it
For the love of the game.

Sam Steel (14)
Honiton Community College, Honiton

The Thunder In The Forest

Thunder, thunder where do you wander?
You shout with fear, you rumble within here.
You mighty shepherd of the sky, why do you scare,
Your rambunctious cries leave me feeling cold and bare.

Suddenly, there's no need to communicate in such a way,
Although you cannot be seen, you can be felt.
You are not just heard, you are smelt,
You are the most dangerous nature some would say.

Where do you hide? Why do you play?
In the darkest forest, that's where,
Within the heavy and twisted vines and long branches,
You do lie...

However
You are not a killer,
You are not a foe,
You are what you are,
A creation within the great sky
that breathes within the darkness of the forest.

Mason Druin Doble (11)
Honiton Community College, Honiton

Historic Moments

H istory is important to me
I t's basically a big
S tory
T ime repeats, some people say,
O r maybe they're just thinking about yesterday
R anching in America and ships that sink
I t's all important and makes you think
C auses of world hunger, we're not doing good

M angoes and melons, we need lots more food
O ranges and apples, but they're all for a cost
M ore and more days are being spent and lost
E nding in us under big lumps of moss
N o, this is it, we're not going to last
T ime will tell our future
S tories will tell our past.

Louisa Jones (13)
Honiton Community College, Honiton

Lightning

The white bolt speeds through the forests of the night
bringing fright to wherever it goes.

The white bolt leaps through the trees of darkness
leaving destruction in its path.

The white bolt pounces through the cold dark sky
its tail leaving a path of light wherever it goes.

The white bolt bites through the trees
their wrath released upon the world below.

The white bolt strikes its prey
with blistering power day on day.

The white bolt's claw slices through the pitch-black night
shredding the skin into bits.

The white bolt...
Speeds through...
The forest of...
The night...

Zac Lancaster (11)
Honiton Community College, Honiton

Lightning

Thunder roars,
Lightning strikes,
All is dead silent tonight

Folks are scared,
Animals are creeping,
All are silent in their homes awaiting
Silent mice scurry home,
Only to find a problem
Everything is destroyed
Homes, villages, cities, countries
All is dead silent tonight.

Everyone, everything,
Is alone,
On the streets,
No home, no food, no water,
Their families dead,
All is dead silent tonight.

All caused
Because of a monster,
A village
An army,
Couldn't stop it,
Leaving everyone, everything
Alone, scared, worried,
All is dead silent tonight.

Emily Rose Ashby (11)
Honiton Community College, Honiton

Soldier

Shoot in the foot, stabbed in the back.
A gun is to kill, a knife is to stab.
The soldier to serve can't ever turn back.
Lives through the night to just be brought back.
Is fighting the answer or never attack?

Gun, a word of meaning to scare off the pack
or maybe a word to ignite attack.
Judgement to forge a better today
or a bluff to cover up nuclear decay.

War. A word of meaning to uprise the pack.
To fight again and never turn back.
But if you find yourself under attack,
by a gun, a war, a naval impact
Just be on the right side and take your shot
because a war is a war whether you like it or not.

Kieran Laker (13)
Honiton Community College, Honiton

Controller

The controller in your hand,
You live the life of the character
You are god,
You make the final leg.

The world is your oyster,
And shape into what you want,
The story you live,
Will make a change in the imaginary world.

The men march in,
Not making a sound,
Come down the buildings,
Which have taken your time.

Use fire versus fire they all say,
The armies that they bring,
Will not survive,
As if you die,
You regenerate.

You march over the bodies,
The final boss is clear,
Now go and win the war,
And finish the story.

Reese Cottington (11)
Honiton Community College, Honiton

A Circus In Black And White

The circus comes and goes
without warning.
No advertisements precede it,
it is simply there...

Illusionists in sweeping gowns
perform to the mesmerised audience,
Causing cards to transform
into doves with the flick of a wrist
or the wave of the hand.

A scent of caramel drifts upon the breeze,
filling the nostrils of the circus goers
as they visit each individual
black and white striped tent,
Contortionists,
Illusionists,
Lion tamers,
Acrobats,
Yet this circus is unique
it is...
A circus in black and white...

Florence Gray (11)
Honiton Community College, Honiton

Nightingale

Pretty, fast
Hazel, launching
Hovering, speckled
Mottled, tawny

Vigorous stalker of the night,
Underworld prowler of the sight.
Sharp piercing silence that damages your ear,
But the only thing you can do is hear

Pretty, fast
Hazel, launching
Hovering, speckled
Mottled, tawny

Amber eyes against the pitch,
Looking behind you for a witch.
Such sleek movements in the pine,
Waiting to hear a devastation whine

Pretty, fast
Hazel, launching
Hovering, speckled
Mottled, tawny.

Cherry Dale (12)
Honiton Community College, Honiton

A Feather's Eyes

Eyes, eyes everywhere
Blue, maybe yellow or green,
The feathers, the feathers of the eyes,
But maybe feathers disguised as eyes.

Flash up then away again,
Just like that,
A click of your fingers,
A wave of a wand,
They're there then gone.

A picturesque display it dances in the sky,
Amazing in all, I was on cloud nine,
The blue, green, yellow and more,
But no matter what, I'm in awe.

A squawk and a flutter
As it flies away
Yet to be seen another day.

Sophie Louise Phillips (12)
Honiton Community College, Honiton

Dreams

They aren't just unreachable fantasies
They are examples of the result of hard work
For anyone who has passion and loves what they want,
It will happen
The only person stopping you
Is you
Anybody with hopes other than a 'normal' life,
have been told to get their heads out of the clouds,
But what's so great about being on the ground?
Your life is your life.
Don't let your only true possession be ruled by someone else.
If you want something,
Get it.

Daniel Loosemore (14)
Honiton Community College, Honiton

Tiger, Tiger

Tiger, tiger burning bright
In the forest's hazy light
To live is an endless fight
Tiger, tiger in the night.

Second biggest of all cats
Hunted for their woolly hats
Tiger, tiger burning bright
Tiger, tiger in the night.

In jungle, in forest
Hunting deer and ferrets
Glowing eyes, sharp claws
Long teeth, gnashing jaws.

Always moving
Ever hungry
As forests are chopped down
The tiger frowns.

Jamie Wallis (11)
Honiton Community College, Honiton

The White Rhino

I know I'm special and
deserve a crown but all I
have now is an ugly
frown and I know I
weigh more than a
a tonne but I sure can run
for miles and miles and
in my crash we splash
and dash in the cool
water under the harsh
African sun but now
we're at the threat of
the hunter's gun, even
though I have a baby
son, he could have had
fun, in the sun like I
used to do.
But now we're on the
run or in a zoo.

Michelle O'Malley (11)
Honiton Community College, Honiton

The Stalker

I was being watched,
Shadowed,
Looked over,
A dark smudge flashed in the corner of my eye,
The one small field looked to go on for miles.
A breeze caught my hair,
A bone-chilling shriek called from behind me,
I turned, but nothing.
I was alone but I knew someone, something was with me,
But what?
The ground rumbled like an earthquake.
I ran but it followed.
I was being...
Stalked.

Zara Maynard (12)
Honiton Community College, Honiton

Strawberry Pirates

There was a bunch of strawberries,
That sailed upon the sea,
They started out with twenty
But now there's only three.

The rest all died of scurvy
Which is crazy cos they're fruit
They made a plan
And wrote it down to divide up all the loot.

They made a map
And wrote it down with an X to mark the spot
In twenty years they'll come back to survive off the lot!

Aaliyah Anna Freeman (11)
Honiton Community College, Honiton

Dance

My spirits rise when I hear the beat,
I have to get up and move my feet,
The rhythm sounds as I leave the ground,
My adrenaline pumping round and round
As I pirouette and turn, my legs feel the burn
Tap, ballet and modern,
All of which I loved to learn!
My hair flicks and flares,
As the audience stares.
I jump so high,
Hoping to reach the sky.
Live, love and just *dance!*

Ruby Drew (11)
Honiton Community College, Honiton

Fish On My Dish

There's fish on my dish
There's fish in the sea
But the fish on my dish are dead you see.

The fish on my dish
Should not be there
But swimming in the sea without a care.

The fish on my dish don't deserve to be caught,
They had a life of their own,
They left behind their family feeling distraught
All that's left of them now is a bone.

Dylan Williams (12)
Honiton Community College, Honiton

Everyone Is Different!

We all have our flaws, everyone is different
People think they know us, everyone is different
By the colour of our skin you think we are bad, everyone is different
A woman is quite sad, everyone is different
You think only men can do the work, everyone is different
Our culture does not define us
Our race does not define us
Our gender does not define us
Everyone is different!

Caleb Freemantle (14)
Honiton Community College, Honiton

Black Blur

A black blur prowling through the night,
Treading softly so it's not to be heard.
Its shimmering black coat shining in the moonlight,
Watching silently, for the creature that it preferred.

Its green eyes staring into the gloom,
Ready to pounce when it's starving.
Getting ready to send its prey to its doom.
Waiting, waiting, waiting.

Jacob Rose (11)
Honiton Community College, Honiton

Darkness

Its darkness will stalk you
A heart of stone
No mortal can overcome it
Its cure unknown
An effect of devastation
Comes from this alone
It strikes during slumber
Attacks your brain
And makes it harder to focus
Every and each day.
The rope is set
You stand on the chair
The end is quick
A ray of light and stairs.

Thomas Cameron Elliott (11)
Honiton Community College, Honiton

The Deathly Scoreboard

As the trees blow, the fires grow,
As the bullets fly, screams shut down and die,
When dying voices are heard, people lose their courage,
But when the horns of battle are blown,
The soldiers rise up, but burn.

The dying light signals the end of a life,
For when they die the counter goes up,
Cornered, no way out, gases surround them,
Cries out for help, only to lose sight and weep,
The toll of the dead rises on the scoreboard.

The days go by, and the nights grow short,
The bodies pile up like seaweed on a shore,
But as the sun comes up with each waking eye,
The guns start up again, for I have been and gone,
I walked the land but now I am done,
But the devil's laugh is heard by all
For the counter keeps rising as the bodies fall.

Reuben Cobb (14)
Kingsley School, Bideford

Almost A Refugee

The noises wouldn't stop,
The guns wouldn't stop,
The bombs wouldn't stop,
The screams wouldn't stop.
Nothing ever stopped.

Then one day,
Some men came
They took Daddy away,
'I will find you,' he said.
They took Mummy away
'I will find you,' she said.

We left that night
My sister and I.
We ran to the fence,
We heard there was a gap,
Anywhere is better than here.

It was quieter near the fence
But we didn't see a gap.

Suddenly...
... My sister screamed behind!
A man with a gun,
Stood holding her arm!
She told me to run,
'I will find you,' she said.

As I turned around;
I heard the haunting sound
And she hit the ground.

Her piercing scream ricocheted
The deafening ricochet.

'I will find you,'
Papa said,
'I will find you,'
Mama said.
'I will find you,'
Sister said.
But now they're all dead.

I almost a refugee;
But now the man's gun
Is pointing at me!

Kitty Lavelle (14)
Kingsley School, Bideford

The Late Trender

He tried to keep up with the trends like a lost bird
He tried to stay with everybody else but he is a nerd
After the trend ends he only just knew about it
After a week he said everything was 'lit'
Everybody thought that he was weird for saying that
Harambe is now dead
And there he is resting on his mannequin challenge scarf on his head
Last week he just downloaded Vine
But every time in the lunch queue he gets pushed out of line
So now he is there still saying things are 'lit'
And there in the playground shouting, 'Just do it!'

Tolly Land (13)
Kingsley School, Bideford

Perfection

Look in the mirror
And what do you see?
An ugly fat girl
or one as skinny as can be?

I'm too fat,
I'm too skinny
I don't look like them
I need to look like them.

You want to look like that?
You want to look perfect?
Feel perfect?
Seem perfect?

You are beautiful
You are healthy
You are amazing
You are perfect

And don't let anyone tell you otherwise.

Amy Macwilliam (13)
Kingsley School, Bideford

Tennis

Tennis is my favourite sport,
It keeps me really fit,
When I step on court,
I know I have to hit
The ball really hard,
With lots of top spin,

So I can keep it in those lines;
Fifteen,
Thirty,
Forty,
Deuce,
Advantage,
Game.

Game is what I like to hear;
Game, set, match!
The next match is important,
Because if I win,
The final is next;

I win!

Rupert George (12)
Kingsley School, Bideford

Sunshine Village

Cold and snowing in the wind
All around the conifer trees,
Noises you can hear are skiers skiing past.
Avalanche patrol throwing TNT to clear the runs,
Dynamite to you and me,
All clear. Time to go.

Ski lifts are starting the morning routine
Cliffs and mountains getting fuller
In the trees children playing snowballs
Igloos are the best place to hide
No one will find you
Got to go to ski school now.

Hugo Wells (11)
Kingsley School, Bideford

Who Am I?

Who am I?

Am I tall? Am I thin?
I have a lot of kin
Am I short? Am I round?
Okay sometimes I horse around.

Am I a nerd or a geek?
I like to follow the chic
Am I strong, am I weak?
I'm not as tough as a hawk's beak.

Am I fast? Am I slow?
I don't really know.
Actually I'm not sure at all,
So that goes back to the first question.

Who am I?

Aaron Smyth (12)
Kingsley School, Bideford

Homework

Homework takes up too much time
So now I'll tell you about it in rhyme.
Homework is cruel
Homework's for a fool
School's for learning
Homework's for burning
Homework is a lie
Homework should die
Homework's not good
Homework could ruin your childhood
Homework's the name of the game
But homework hurts my brain
So take it from me,
Homework, it's not meant to be.

Ben Hansen (12)
Kingsley School, Bideford

The Judo Fight

It's the smell of the mat...
It's the cheer of my family,
It's the sweat that you get
In a judo fight!

It's the fun on the bus,
On the way to the fight.
Being on the podium makes me feel tall,
And getting a medal makes me feel cool.

The clink of the medals
Is the sound of a good fight!
But we learn more from the losing
So that's also alright!

Harry Lucas (12)
Kingsley School, Bideford

Sport

People love it,
People hate it,
People play it,
People rate it,
People smash it,
People wing it,
People fling it,
People cheer it,
Crowds love it,
Even scream it,
Whilst wearing their own team's kit.
Newspapers cover it,
Radio 5 Live reports it,
Olympians unite it.
People love it,
People hate it.
The world's a better place for it.

Poppy Goaman (12)
Kingsley School, Bideford

But You Still Don't Know Who You Are

Have you ever woken up and not got out of bed,
because every magazine and book you've ever read
Teaches you to look in the mirror and want to be dead,
But you still don't know who you are?

Have you ever been in a room full of people singing and dancing,
And you're sitting in the corner, your brain is romancing
About how your teenage brain is being attracted
To people you first thought were enchanting
But you still don't know who you are?

Have you ever looked in a mirror and seen a you
That's warped and inflated and split in two
And they don't understand why you're not eating food
But the you that you see makes real you feel blue
But you still don't know who you are?

Have you ever been aware something's wrong in your brain
And it won't go away, you think you're going insane?
It keeps coming back, again and again
It repeats in your head like a silly refrain
But you still don't know who you are.

Have you had no clue on Earth, what you are, what you'll be
And no clue on Earth what could fill you with glee.
So you hope, and you wish and you pray desperately
But if only you could see the you that I see,
Because you just might then know who you are.

Zoë Clutterbuck (12)
Rednock School, Dursley

I Have A Pound Coin

I have a pound coin
And if I save up
There will be millions of things that I can get.

So I have a pound coin,
And if I save up,
I can get a Lego set,
Or a new model of a superhero,
Or I can get a ray jet,
Or a new game made of ones and zeros.
Or I could get a remote control car,
That I can move from afar.

So I have a pound coin,
And if I really save up,
I can get a new games console
With tonnes of new ways to control.
Or I can get a new phone,
Or even a flying drone.
Or I can get a new TV
So I can watch the BBC.

So I have a pound coin,
And if I really saved up.
Then I could just buy the shop.
But none of that will happen
Because my pound has gone to charity,
For those who really need it.

Because I can get a pound coin
And I can save up easily
But those in need can't
And they need our help.
Owen Dennis Dyas Jones (12)
Rednock School, Dursley

Friendship

When you're young and have friends,
If it's ten or if it's two,
You'll have fallouts, arguments,
The rest of us do too!

There'll be one or two great ones,
Who will always be there,
You tell them everything about you,
And they'll listen and care!

Secrets you'll tell them,
And they'll tell you theirs too,
Respect's always there between them and you,
Because you've got their back and they've got theirs too.

There will always be those that go behind your back,
Say they're your friend when they're not,
That's when you remember just one simple thing,
All of the friends that you've got!

Know that whatever the weather; be it rain or shine
There'll always be that one friend you love, trust and admire,
Because no matter what happens in the end
You can always turn to a friend!

Natasha Trinder (13)
Rednock School, Dursley

Judge

People sometimes say to stay away from people who are black
That they'll only turn round later to stab you in the back.

And people sometimes say that all white people think they're the best
That from head to toe they're high above the rest.

And people walk past people covered in tattoos
But you can't just assume, that they're high and on the booze.

You can't go around sticking tags on people's chests,
It honestly just shows you think you're better than the rest.

Everyone is different, we all have our flaws,
You can't just assume and go peering in people's doors.

Something more important than anything else,
Don't judge people, you might find they're a little like yourself.

Alice Smith (12)
Rednock School, Dursley

Bully

Come to school, dreading the day
Scared of what the bully will say
Awake all night
Scared with fright.

That's it, I've had enough
Time to grow up and be tough
I'll tell the teacher
I'll tell my friends
This is where the bullying ends.

You can't have my money
You can't have my lunch,
That's it, you bully
It's come to the crunch.

No more pinching, punching or fights,
I've had enough sleepless nights,
I'm not scared of what you say,
I want to enjoy my school day.

That's told her, free at last
I'm gonna forget all that's past.
Bullying is not big, it's not clever
We should all be friends and get on together.

Charlotte Morse (12)
Rednock School, Dursley

Her Nose, Her Eyes, Her Body

I took a selfie of me with my friends,
I thought I looked fine,
With my hair in a bun and no make-up on,
But soon the comments came rolling in,
'Too many fries, why aren't you thin?'
There was even one which said
'Follow @*** now she is a real girl'

I took it to heart
I know I shouldn't have
But looking at her perfect nose, thin and long,
Her perfect eyes,
Round and sweet with lashes long enough to paint a masterpiece
Then I looked at her perfect body
Thin waist, wide hips and polished skin
As well as lips
They had a shine
It was nothing like mine,
Nothing like me,
She was something I could never be.
because the only person like me, is me.

Cara Pickard (12)
Rednock School, Dursley

Bullying

Don't let people judge you by your looks
And your pictures,
Make sure if you get bullied you tell your
Snitchers
Don't listen to those people out there,
That judge you because of your hair,
That like to give you an evil snare,
That hate to breathe your air,
Who despise you and are horrible,
As they think you're terrible,
Don't be afraid to tell someone,
That will help you through everyone,
Who are mean,
And green,
And don't know what to think,
As their dresses are pink
Be who you want to be,
And be free,
Don't be afraid to follow your dreams,
As you could join a hockey team,
So don't let people judge you,
As you are who you are.

Isabella Delrosa (12)
Rednock School, Dursley

Stranded Deep

As I stare up to the surface
With no reason or no purpose,
I feel like I'm stranded
Upon that sandy shore.

The beaches and mouldy coconuts
The boiling sun with dry deserts,
And all I needed was that flight
So I could be safe.

As I sink into the water
I feel like I'm falling,
Into a pit of darkness
As it creeps up behind me.

I'm starting to lose my sight
Because it's beginning to turn night,
And I'm trying to hold my breath
But it's just not working.

My head is now pounding
'Cause I fret that I am drowning,
I must rest my head
On the soft seabed floor.

Hollie Jean Walton (12)
Rednock School, Dursley

Best Friends

We were best friends
But then you changed,
Something about you seemed strange,
I didn't like it that way!

We were best friends,
You acted differently at school,
But over text you didn't care!

We were best friends,
You spoke about me to others,
You acted like I wasn't there, like I didn't exist!

We were best friends,
I didn't do anything to you,
But somehow you must have thought I did!

We were best friends,
I thought you did it for attention,
You did it for someone else, and you wouldn't
Know how that made me feel.

Scarlett Maule (12)
Rednock School, Dursley

Homework?

Homework brings such hatred in me,
But there's nothing we can do,
The government has decided on the rules,
It will stick with us like glue!

Homework is a big disaster,
To me and everyone;
It's never going to leave this world,
So let's try and get it done!

Homework doesn't spark up our lives,
It's every child's fear;
Whilst wicked teachers set more and more,
Dear! Oh dear! Oh dear!

Homework, it is a terrible thing,
Who invented it?
Life is going from bad to worse,
I think I just want to quit!

Nathan Curry (11)
Rednock School, Dursley

Foxes

Paws pattering,
Leaves scattering,
Animals snoozing,
Children losing,
In autumn races.

Laces,
Happy faces,
Happy life,
Preparing food with a knife,
Children hiding behind rocks.

Have you seen the fox?
A beautiful creature with orange fur,
Hiding with her,
His mate,
People kill and hate.

They run,
Not for fun,
They run from fear,
Faster than a deer,
Bang...
Bang...
Bang...

They fall...
Humans are cruel,
Horrible creatures,
When it comes to hunting.

Alanah Williams (12)
Rednock School, Dursley

Death

There is one word that is hated by millions,
One word that everyone is thinking about,
One word that could never be forgotten,
Death!

Death is a word that could make anyone cry,
It's a word that most of us try and ignore,
But when someone close to you dies,
It's like a black hole sucking up the happy memories!

The thought of never seeing someone again is horrible.
No one could tell you how much it hurts when someone close to you dies.
Don't think people live forever,
Take every adventure thrown at you,
And be yourself.

Charlotte Tuckwell (13)
Rednock School, Dursley

Too Many Adverts!

There are too many adverts on TV
About fast food, PPI and obesity.
Then comes on your favourite show
But soon, later, it has to go.

They come on with the theme tunes,
Just advertising honeymoons
To get you to explore
The wonderful outdoors.

They tell you about your data
Or about your local baker.
Saving the world's nature
Or talking to your neighbour.

This may seem strange to think about
But this is something that needs a shout.

Harrison Page (11)
Rednock School, Dursley

Stars And Cars

Stars and cars,
They're there and then they're gone.
They hide and ride,
Pinpricks in the sky.

Endless places and names,
Even more wishes and dreams,
Spotted only by a few,
Are engravings of the truth.

Clusters and constellations,
In much earnest we search,
But hiding from our eyes,
Blinding fires in disguise.

We're all stars and cars,
We're here and then we're gone,
We hide and ride,
We remember.

Millie Young (12)
Rednock School, Dursley

Keep Your Friends Close

Keep your friends close,
You never know when your friendship is coming to a close,
Maybe you were best friends the other day,
But now you're just waiting to fall away,
Keep your friends close.

So now it's just history,
Perhaps it wasn't meant to be,
I remember those days when we'd just play,
But now it's different and I just want to say,
Keep your friends close.

I hope we can be friends again!

Holly Morris (12)
Rednock School, Dursley

Similar

Emma is short,
Sam is tall,
Louise self-harms because of school.

Callum is big,
Lucy is thin,
Sally has scars and loose, baggy skin.

Oscar binge eats,
Molly's anorexic,
She eats a lot then makes herself sick.

Emelie is rich,
Ella is poor,
Josh has policemen knocking at his door.

Everyone is similar,
Tall, big or thin,
Because all of their hearts are still beating.

Amy Winfield (13)
Rednock School, Dursley

Friendship

F riends are forever, they
R eally care about you
I love them,
E ven though they can be annoying
N othing can break our friendship
D o not try to break our friendship, because
S ome friendships are meant to last forever
H opefully we will never fall out because
I have a really good bond with these girls, there have never been any
P eople more important to me than them.

Mia Richardson (11)
Rednock School, Dursley

2016

In Paris there was a suicide bomb
Thirty more lives gone.

There was a presidential election
But people weren't voting on logic, they were voting on affection.

Russia was caught drugging
Olympic titles they were mugging.

Refugees tried to cross the border
They tried to escape slaughter.

A football team's plane crashed
Their legacy was smashed!

Charlie Utting (11)
Rednock School, Dursley

Bear Poem

Shackled beast surrounded in chains
Whilst he stood there hopeless and useless
Whipped with ropes, unbearable pain,
Whilst people around him were being a nuisance.

If only I could talk, thought the bear
You could hear my feelings and care.
Should he cry or shout?
All he wants to do is get out.

Standing still, broken, lost
Sore and stiff, no mercy to cost.

Lizzy Dunn (11)
Rednock School, Dursley

Why Friends Are Like A Box Of Chocolates

Friends, friends, we all have them.
Shoulders to lean on, secrets to be shared
Full of heart, compassion, joy and care.

We all have them, they are our companions,
So share them, enjoy them and make everyone count.

Friends, friends, we all have them.
But they're better than chocolates
because they are for life.

James Moir (11)
Rednock School, Dursley

Love

Love is one of those things,
That no one really knows about.
It's not a shape or a colour,
But it's the way you feel about someone.
You can't see, hear or touch it,
But you can feel it right down deep.
It's what you feel for me
And that's what really counts.

Lauren Whittaker (12)
Rednock School, Dursley

Hibernate

Little hedgehog tiny and small
Does not make any noise at all
But every six months
Winter will appear
Time for this hedgehog to round up his gear
Round up his den
All nice and snug
Comfy and cosy
And tired tonight
Goodbye little hedgehog
And have a good night.

Courtney Phillips (11)
Rednock School, Dursley

President's Inauguration Day 2017

If I was the most powerful person in the world, I would:

Stop the wars in Aleppo and Syria and let all the families live in peace and make it peaceful.
Stop people littering and polluting the world and get them caught.
Make people have a better life and let them live in nice houses if they don't.
Stop people being homeless and make more homeless shelters for them and give them homes.
Stop terrorists attacks and send the army out to stop them invading England.
Stop gangs in the world and stop children getting involved and getting hurt.
Find a cure for cancer and let people live longer.
Make a taxi firm in all villages so that people can get from A to B.
Stop racism against black and white people in foreign countries and in England.
Make places to live in for people who don't have nice places to live in.
Give everyone a nice life so that they're not surrounded by wars and guns.
For people who do not have any money, help them open a bank account and get food and drink
Help people get back on track and not let them go back down hill and keep an eye on them
Let everyone enjoy life and make every day count because you don't know what the future holds for you!

Kieran Playne (12)
Saltash.Net Community School, Saltash

It Is Not So Bad As I Thought It Would Be

Everything was fine and it's not so bad now.
When Mum and Dad were together,
Me and my sister used to do things like go on holidays
and go places like ice skating, swimming, shopping,
Jump, Plymouth, Spain, which was really hot
and had a swimming pool
and last of all was skiing in December 2015.
Everything changed when we got back.
The day Dad left, he went to darts
and Mum said that Dad has to go and live somewhere else
And he is not coming back.
I don't know how to fix it.
I went to school but couldn't do my work
and I didn't feel like playing.
It's been over a year now and this is how it is.
It is not so bad as I thought it would be.
I've got two families with two Christmases,
two birthdays and two Easters, with Dad over the weekends.
I sleep better at Mum's in my own bed.

Mia Kenworthy (12)
Saltash.Net Community School, Saltash

The Death Of Patrick

Welcome to the Edwardian times and a house by the river,
Who lives in the house?
A teenage boy called Patrick and his uncle.
Patrick's parents died when he was one,
So his uncle brought him up.

Patrick was a dirty boy, because he was a blacksmith.
His uncle was quite rich as he was a banker.

One afternoon, his uncle was rocking in his rocking chair
When suddenly, he dropped dead!
Patrick came home and saw him in his chair which was still rocking!
Before Patrick could inherit his uncle's house and money,
A nosy neighbour
Told everyone that he saw Patrick put poison in his uncle's food.

Patrick went to court, was found guilty of murder
And he was hanged.

The real murderer, his twin brother, Peter,
Laughed as he counted his uncle's money!

Daniel Collins (14)
Saltash.Net Community School, Saltash

What Might Stop Me?

I want to be a builder
when I grow up
and build my house in the middle of nowhere
so it will be quiet
so my car won't get scratched by kids
because they won't pay for the damage
it might cost a lot.
There might be things that stop me.

My dream car is a Nissan GTR.
When I grow up I will build my own garage in the middle of nowhere
so it will be quiet
so then it won't get scratched by little kids
and I am doing it on my own.
There might be things that stop me.

My dream is to ride a KTM
and I might make a bike track
so me and my family can ride in the middle of nowhere
so then it will be fun.
There might be things that stop me.
What might stop me is my wife
when she says you are not doing that!

I'm only fourteen
and I know what might stop me
I know what I want to do.
The main thing to stop me is me.
I give up easily.
I nearly gave up writing this.

Ryan Coulson (14)
Saltash.Net Community School, Saltash

Why When Will You Get A Life

When I tell my family they don't understand.
I tell them I can't clean my fingernails
Because the worm is homeless if they do!
They call me lazy, they just don't understand.
My worms have names
And I talk to the worms,
Jim Bob, Jeff 21, Bob 21, Bobby, Gary
And the Majestic Eagle.
Three of my fingers are called No Jeff,
No Gary and No Jon.

Jeff 21 and Jim Bob play football with Gary
Under my nails and use one of my
Blood cells as a football.

Also they don't understand me
When I play Pokémon TC Go Trading
Card games only on PC.
They said, 'I need to get a life.'
But they don't understand
Because in my Pokémon world
It is my reality, not only a game on PC.

Jack Hawes (11)
Saltash.Net Community School, Saltash

News

In the city there was a news van going into a dark
alley in the streets
Two men scratched the news van and backed up
out of the alley.
The two men drove to the airport to get a helicopter
to follow the news van to the news street
to tell the news station all about what happened
in the world
so they can tell the world don't panic in the streets.
The world is changing.
The news will keep you up to date.
The war was changing.
The lives were changing.
The cars and the shops were changing.
The streets were changing.
The news will keep you up to date,
Tell the world don't panic in the streets.

Thomas Kinver (14)
Saltash.Net Community School, Saltash

Recipe Of Happiness

2 bags of arts and crafts
1 packet of love music
2g of sweet hearts
1 bag of love
2kg of ice cream
2 bags of Katy Perryness
2 cups of joyful friendship
3 bags of hard workers
1 dash of feeling kind to each other
½ spoonful of caring for friends
1 bag of loving children
2kg of maths and English
1 bag of lollipops
2kg of sweetness
1 bag of candy
½ bag of learning times tables
1 bag of dancing with a group of friends
4 drops of sharing with dancers
2 bags of nice without Popski eating my homework
In any order!

Megan Slocombe (15)
Saltash.Net Community School, Saltash

Just Thoughts That Often Come Into My Head

Just thoughts that often come into my head
Mum... loving, caring, kind
Music... I hate it, too loud
Pencil... I hate it because I have to work
Book... I don't like reading my reading book out loud
Rubber... I rub out my mistakes
Phone... I only speak to my best friends
Earrings... these are special because I got them for Christmas
Car... I think about my birthday outing
Drink... I don't like water
Headphones... I wear my headphones to play on my tablet to get space
Dad... loving, hardworking
Swimming... I can't swim
Dog... I want a dog
Friends... my friends are sweet and kind
Home... warm and hectic!

Jess Burgess (11)
Saltash.Net Community School, Saltash

My Chair

Words come into my head
Play - outside with my friends and family
Now - always being told to hurry up
Mum - kindness and embarrassing kisses
Late
Cat - annoying cat keeps scratching me
Happy - excited about my birthday
Car - I think about my birthday
Pen
My family
Running - we're normally running away from Tom
Dog - I think about if I had a dog
Music - I hate music
Nan - loving, caring, kind but not kind to Grandad
Room - watching TV
Phone - I only speak to my best friends
Chair - I sit on my chair and think
Late again!

Laura Hackworthy (12)
Saltash.Net Community School, Saltash

Recipe For Madness V Recipe For Anger

1 bag of sugar
2 cups of children's tears
2lbs of wheelchairs
1½ cups of monkeys
1 cup of turtles
2 spoonfuls of salt
1 dash of puppets
4 drops of saltwater
And 1 packet of dragonflies
V
1 bag of
2 cups of
2lbs of
½ cup of
2 spoonfuls of
1 dash of
4 drops of
And 1 packet of
Well actually, I don't know
It just turns on
And off with the help of
A cup of tea
And a calm space to be on
My own for a while,
Under a cushion or table.

Elliot Jordan (14)
Saltash.Net Community School, Saltash

President's Inauguration Day

If I was the most powerful person in the world,

I would stop world wars
Everyone would have the right to speak
Everyone would get paid the same
I would set new laws
Everyone would be retaking their driving test every two years
All would drive on the same side of the road or £300 fine
Animal welfare. Newborn baby animals would stay with their mum until they're on solid food.

Thomas Perry (15)
Saltash.Net Community School, Saltash

New Baby Brother

I don't mind
I don't mind if he is crying
I don't like Mum being ill
I don't like my brothers coming in my room
I don't mind if he is crying
Only a week to go until he is born!
I'll give him cuddles to cheer him up
so long as he doesn't grow up to be a brother who comes into my room without asking!
I hope my Mum gets better soon as he is born.

Connor Laker (13)
Saltash.Net Community School, Saltash

Recipe For Anger

1 bag of chores
2 cups of being alone
2kg of Mum's help when she could do it herself
½ cup of doing washing
2 spoons of madness when I'm not allowed on my iPad
1 dash of homework
Easy to find calm in my imagination.
I don't mind really.
Just sometimes being a carer is hard.

Erin Jordan (12)
Saltash.Net Community School, Saltash

Recipe For Depression

1 cup of no family
500g of dead animals
20ml of no home
9 cups of children's salty tears
2 years of drugs for heart problems
Even when I have had my heart operation
50 years of no Dr Who
20 years stuck at school
50ml of cats biting me
A black bin bag full of this.

Oscar Price (16)
Saltash.Net Community School, Saltash

A Recipe For Anger

1 bag of my cat attacking me
2 cups of anger from brothers
2kg of my brother taking my sweets
½ cup of dogs barking all the time
2 spoonfuls of cats fighting
1 dash of muddy paw prints over my duvet
4 drops of telly on the wrong channel
And 1 packet of Dad's music!

Saffron Paice (15)
Saltash.Net Community School, Saltash

President's Inauguration Day

If I was the most powerful person in the world...

Children would be able to stay up for as long as they wanted
Everyone would lie in bed till 10 every morning (if they wanted to)
Everyone would have to like Beyblades!
There would be no such thing as Maths!
Everyone would have to keep healthy.

Matthew Pean (13)
Saltash.Net Community School, Saltash

Recipe For Sadness And Happiness

1 cup of grumpiness
2 cups of fighting with my brothers over nothing
½ cup of being alone
¼ of stupidness of my brothers
2tbsp of shouting at my brothers
½ cup of crying
Happiness when we playing together
laughing and loving as always.

Daisy Lane (12)
Saltash.Net Community School, Saltash

Freedom

Lady is my pony a 13.3 liver chestnut
She loves people and snorts for attention,
We both love hacking which is where we're going now.
Her coat was gleaming and my boots were shining,
We were raring to go and ready to ride.
The horse box pulled up and Lady was loaded,
Onto the lorry we were almost there, the horse box slowed down and ground to a halt.
We were tacked up in no time with my hat on my head
With one quick jump I was up onto her back.
The next thing I knew I was trotting down the drive
As we got to the gate I opened it wide
Now we're up on Black Down and ready to run,
The view was wonderful, you can see for miles.
The rolling hills blend in with the sky,
The whole world is stretched out before me,
And white fluffy clouds bobbing so high.
Lady knew what was happening and was jogging quite fast.
With a gentle squeeze of my heels we galloped across the open hills
With the wind in my hair and blowing her mane into my face,
I crouched low over her neck like a jockey in a race
This is what I'd wanted for such a long time,
I laughed out loud as we were galloping along the hilltops.

Evie Ward (12)
Sidcot School, Winscombe

The Barn Owl

In amongst the tree it swoops,
Ears poised;
Eyes alert.
Dusk is coming quickly,
The night is ever falling.
But this being does not mind, no flee the darkness, instead it relishes.
For it is a barn owl.

As the glowing sun sinks below the dark horizon,
The owl drifts among the twilight,
Its regal wings forming eerie shadows in the last streak of pale light;.
But soon the earth is engulfed in veils of darkness,
Heeding not the bird, as it sails above the ground in the still air -
For it is a barn owl.

The darkness is now fully set,
Everything is quiet,
Everything still.
As humans slumber in their beds,
The barn owl reigns over the earth,
Its wings glinting, in the silvery moonlight,
Eyes shining and sparkling in the darkness of the night.

It does not fear;
It is not ruled by doubt or dread,
For it is a barn owl.

All too soon the pale glimpses of first light return,
The darkness waning in the stead of morning reign.
And with it the barn owl must go
It belongs not, in a world of day and turmoil
A day full of noise and smell
The stillness and darkness of night is its realm,
For it is a barn owl.

The greyness of dawn breaks upon the earthen landscape,
A chorus of birdsong resonating through the air,
The night is slowly retreating
And with it the bird must flee,
As it turns and swoops with powerful wings, for the safety of entwined trees,
The first stream of life-giving light, shine upon the bird
A beak now tinged with the rust of blood,
Talons clenched in fists of prey
Evidence of a hard night's hunt,
To which it will return.
For it is a barn owl.

Hannah Peters (14)
Sidcot School, Winscombe

The Race

Take your marks, *beep!*
The cold water hits your face,
A million pins hit your cheeks.

The sound drowns out,
Everything goes blurry,
Then you remember;
This is a race.

First the underwater kick,
Not knowing who's in front;
Not knowing if you're in front.

Then you surface,
Take your first breath,
No time to think.
Thinking costs time...

First 50:
You feel great,
I can do this.

Second 50:
Your lungs are crying for air.
Your throat burns,
A blazing fire, flickers at your uvula.

Third 50:
The eternal battle inside your head.
Your body screams for you to stop,
Your brain says, 'Go faster!
Keep your head down. Don't breathe!'

Last 50:
You're nearly there.
Your body is dead.
Any scrap of energy you have left, you use.
Your technique is appalling, but you don't care.

Everything is fixated on the wall.
It's getting closer but you're still not there.
Last five metres, head down, don't breathe.
You hit the timing pad with as much force as you can muster.

Immediately your head turns to look at the board,
A new best time.
You start to relax,
Happiness gushes through your body;
Like opening the curtains on a sunny day.

All the 5am starts,
The months of commitment,
The hours of hard work,
The many parties you have missed,
Are all worth it.

Maggie Hammond (13)
Sidcot School, Winscombe

Seasons

Here I sit in the summer,
And I see blue skies,
Fluffy clouds drifting across the baby-blue sky,
Trees full of leaves,
With a little breeze,
A couple of sweet birds tweet in the trees,
As I open my window I feel a sudden rush of warmth,
The sweet smell of summer,
I feel refreshed.

Here I sit in the autumn,
And I see a grey sky,
With the green grass slowly dying,
And brown and orange leaves covering the lawn like a blanket,
In all the fields I see greedy sheep munching the grass,
I hear the rain lashing against the window like an angry piano player,
I feel the rush of freezing air coming through the window.

Here I sit in the winter,
As I look up I see nothing but white sky,
As I sit in front of the fire watching the snowflakes dancing outside my window
In my warmest onesie
And hot chocolate with whipped cream and mini marshmallows.

Here I sit in the spring,
And I see some blue sky,
With the fresh green grass growing,
I see young lambs loving life,
I see the farmer with his sheep dog in his red tractor,
All the trees bursting back to life,
I feel excited from all the chocolate the Easter Bunny gave me.

Elsa Kerstin Cardale (11)
Sidcot School, Winscombe

Death's Dark Corners

One by one,
Over the hill they come.

Boots a-thumping
Torches a-blazing

Eyes and hearts down,
Never wanting to feel the shame.

Death making his way up through the village,
Snaking around his workers.

As he passes, the lights go out,
And blood runs cold.

No more safe places or
Hiding spaces.

Hands over mouths;
They wait.

Mothers with small children
Streaks running down their dusty faces.

Whispering prayers to loved ones.
Hoping they knew.

One stops,
The others run ahead.

But fill the space in front of him
Like a swarm.

He feels Death's fingers
Reaching, constricting.

Snaking his way through his molecules
Making each one dormant and stiff.

His knees fall
His eyes roll back.

This is to pay
The debt I have made.

Lucy Zeeman (13)
Sidcot School, Winscombe

The Conflict We Face

The planes that soared above our heads,
The tanks that crushed our creaking beds.
The bombs that smashed windows from afar,
The guns that sent splintered doors ajar.

The vulture that glided in the distant sky,
The raven that looked me in the eye.
The lonely magpie that sat on the wall,
The owl with its talons, long and tall.

The crowded court rooms, ancient and old,
The shocking stories that were always told.
The politicians that stood, ammo at the ready,
The words that punctured, but fell like confetti.

The people who followed delicate like the snow,
The people who fought, stronger than we know.
The people who tore us apart like soft sand,
The people who brought us together to stand.

The conflict we face is anything but kind,
The rest that comes after brings us all peace of mind.
The war that we hate is the war that we make,
But the more war we make.
The more lives we take.

Ruby Cogan (13)
Sidcot School, Winscombe

Our Earth

To go back to our world before urbanisation,
Before the torrent of civilisation.
To swim in oceans so pure and blue,
To observe a world without me or you.
To marvel at landscapes that seem to never end,
Without knowing that a city is just round the bend.
To watch animals wander and wander,
Not having to worry 'bout what's over yonder.

To hear the wind whisper through the trees,
And be engulfed by its sweet harmonies.
To hear the sound of splashing waves,
Long before humans emerged from their caves.
To taste the crisp, fresh, natural air,
Not spoilt by men without a care.

Just because we want everything in one go,
We shouldn't use Earth's resources in one fell blow.
The world's welfare should concern those in power,
Though climate change doesn't exist inside of Trump Tower.

Ultimately, there must be a solution
To all this destroying human pollution.

Sarah Carr (14)
Sidcot School, Winscombe

The Forgotten Holocaust (Namibia 1890 - 1915)

Sail or walk
Around the isle.
You'll never know what's inside.
Corpses scattered throughout a paradise.
Dead. They didn't even try to hide.

'Waste no compassion on these people'
'They're savages, it's easy to see'
'For their skin is darker than our own'
'And they speak not like you or me.'

The rifles of the Schuztruppe
The sword of the Kaiser himself.
We cut down these savages,
Enslave their families.
End their suffering
Not one savage shall remain
Not one shall be given help.

And the child, crying fearfully.
The wounded left for dead.
The proud chief, now a coward's slave
The settlement doused in red
How could we forgive this slaughter?
How could we forget?

But alas,
We have forgotten this Holocaust of old.
The victims gone,
The killers buried,
A deadly secret, never to be told.

James Barber (14)
Sidcot School, Winscombe

Riots

Riots raid the streets,
Destroying people's homes,
As death starts to greet,
Snapping people's bones.

Petrol bombs explode,
Gunshots rack the air,
Guns start to overload,
Men as vicious as some bears.

Blood is everywhere,
Dead bodies littered around,
Screams are piercing the air,
The air full of horrible sound.

Death is taking over,
There is no chance of survival,
A man who looks like an ogre,
Is helping Death's arrival.

He starts to shoot men down,
No one stands a chance,
He makes his way through town,
Not taking a second glance.

People die by the minute,
Bodies falling to the ground,
There is no such thing as a limit,
To the death that's flying around.

Suddenly, the riots stop,
Not a sound is heard,
The silence continues without a stop
Not even the sound of a bird.

Luca Cuckson (11)
Sidcot School, Winscombe

War

Why is war a thing?

Why must we fight over a little argument?
An argument that leads to war,
Which after all the pain and suffering ends in death?
Every death means a family in the world,
Getting a tiny little letter telling them their child has died.
All these thoughts surround their heads,
They're never going to speak to them,
They're never going to hug them...
They're never going to see them again.
All of those brave and willing soldiers may have been 19 or 20,
But to their parents they were still small and defenceless,
They are gone forever,
Forever seems way too long but they have to get used to it.

But... somehow it feels impossible,
It seems like it's all a prank,
All some sort of joke,
And they're going to jump out at you and shout 'surprise'...
But they never do.
Their child will never walk through that door.

Mackensie Jones (12)
Sidcot School, Winscombe

Why Are You Missing?

Shadows lay under the silver moon, as the sun begins to rise,
As I lay in the glistening light I remember the prize,
The prize of a lifetime,
The only problem - there was one person missing,
Springtime.

Crowds gather vastly to show appreciation,
I wept in the corner of the little nation,
Winter was here with no intent to stop,
Springtime was gone with no intention to swap.

Why was it difficult to face winter?
Imagine a person tortured by a splinter,
Missing I know, I would never forget,
The one true love I first met.

Cold spluttered everywhere back in reality
Life-long memories seemed a mortality,
When would this regret end?
I knew it was my fault but I didn't think it would bend.

You're now missing. I'm in regret,
I'm sorry, I lost the bet.

Hannah Fairley (14)
Sidcot School, Winscombe

Vale

I get into the car.
One last look back,
All my friends waving
I want to collapse
Shutting the door
Tears on my face
I'm not dreaming
I'm awake.

On my way to the airport,
Looking at the sights
Knowing it might be the last time
Hating every moment
Tears still falling
And fear building up like a terrible warning.

Get to the airport
Know I won't stay long.
Have to say bye,
One last time
Fearing the other side,
Leaving after a long time,
Made my home.
Made my nest,
Will there be anything left.

No one smiling
All I see is crying
Thinking of a new path
That I will make
Will there be a future
Or will I have to wait?

Moving on
No choice but to go
I have a life other than at home.

Isabella Hoddell (12)
Sidcot School, Winscombe

A Simple Worldwide Conflict

The world begins,
Nothing to worry about but you and your kin.

You meet another, similar to you.
Where, what and why, more importantly who?

Now you watch; for hours on end.
Are they foe, or are they friend?

They speak, they write
To share their opinion rather than fight.

Alas, they are not your views
And for this, they'll pay their dues.

You look at them; they don't belong,
So you say simply, 'Your views, are wrong...'

Both so adamant that you each are right.
You find a simple solution. A simple fight.

All this to protect your kin
Now - war begins...

Jacob Perry (14)
Sidcot School, Winscombe

The Bright Light

The bright light in the night,
How strange your embers burn!
To remain the purest white,
In wait for day's return.

When the wind blows hard,
You struggle to keep your flame.
And when your timber is charred,
Then would you tame.

As your hearth begins to cool,
Do you feel your light fade?
Soon you exhaust your fuel,
It seems your fate is made.

The morning sky flashes,
Your light becomes one of many.
Amongst your tepid ashes,
Are the remnants of what used to be.

The day turns to a night,
Your fire is restored once more.
You remain a purest white,
A bright light in the night.

Jim Mitchell (14)
Sidcot School, Winscombe

It's Not Your Fault

I know you tried your best
And I hope that you are well
I won't be here with you
One day you will join me.

But now I shall go to the greater place.
I don't want to live...

When I am gone please remember me,
The child that loved you,
I will not see you
It's for the greater good.

They don't like me
They are horrid
They bully me
But they won't any more.

Then I got support
I was able to be positive,
I was able to have fun,
So now I must thank them...

William Sandiford (12)
Sidcot School, Winscombe

Kittens

Jumping, pouncing, scratching and licking,
That's what they do all day,
Chase, climbing, purring and rolling,
Their mother is trying to sleep for she has had enough for today,
The kittens are full of mischief and fun,
When will they sleep and stop their play?
They like eating fish and chasing mice
Cuddling their owner is like being in paradise!
As day is dawning,
The kittens are yawning,
Goodnight little kittens,
We'll see you in the morning!

Claudia Jarman (11)
Sidcot School, Winscombe

Art

What is art,
But creation of the heart?
Strokes of brushes,
Inky rushes,
Of fiction, just a part.
Capturing reality,
Of life and love; a clarity.
A great new world without a fee,
The candle in the dark.
Explosions of colour of clay and wood,
The perfect image, always good,
Make anything you dream you could,
Because what is art,
But creation of the heart?

Amelia Carveth (14)
Sidcot School, Winscombe

Words Hurt

The careless comments that cursed me every day
Were the weapons which almost took my life away.
The worlds that scarred me like a tattoo,
A permanent reminder of what I meant to you.

I thought that you cared, that you were my friend,
You would protect me and on you I would depend.
But that wasn't how our story unfurled,
You showed your true colours, you ruined my world.

Nothing was good enough, no words I could say,
My actions were futile and you made me pay.
No bruises, no evidence, nothing to see,
No one ever noticed, all oblivious to me.

But inside my head, I felt worthless and used,
I wanted to shout, say how I felt.
To shout, 'Words do hurt!' they cut as deep as a knife,
That words such as yours, might take my life.

'You're worthless, you're nothing, you're nothing to me'
Those words strike a resonance too deep to ever see
Just like bruises might heal, but the scars remain,
You try to move on but still feel the pain.

The careless comments that cursed me every day,
Were the weapons which almost took my life away.
But now I know I have to much to live for,
I'm worthy, I'm me, and your words won't hurt me any more.

Abby Middlebrooke (14)
St Peter's CE (A) School, Exeter

Don't Become A Caged Bird

Don't become a caged bird
Jailed by society
When all you see becomes blurred
From the tears and anxiety

Don't hide back in the shell
Of who you used to be
Why put yourself through hell
To become your own bully

You could fly above the fear
If you weren't afraid to fall
Come on, you're so near
The sky can hear your call

The biggest enemy to your dreams
Is the demon in your mind
Nothing is really what it seems
Sooo, has the world gone blind?

Can't you see the problem
With seeing all the bad?
Really we are all awesome
And that is what is so sad

How are we supposed to feel
When society has turned so strange?
Someone needs to take the wheel
And make a worldwide change

Busta Rhyme - The South West

It is the worst form of torture
To believe you aren't enough
You can be your greatest supporter
And you don't have to act all tough

Again you wear your fake smile
Painted on your old mask
Too scared to try a new hairstyle
But what's to lose, I ask?

You will get it wrong sometimes
And maybe make a mistake
But you don't have any more lifetimes
So give yourself a break

And if you feel you're drowning
In the madness and the hate
Look up at that mountain,
Look back down and choose your fate

Make it whatever you desire
Impossible it may seem
But it will only raise you higher
To one day reach that dream

Don't let the greatest monster
Always hold you back
It may be the hardest to conquer
As self-believe is what you lack

Don't be dismayed
It is never too late
To stop being afraid
And turn into something great!

Alice Dean (14)
St Peter's CE (A) School, Exeter

Respect

You call her names as she runs by
Hiding her face, she withholds her sigh.
Laughing, jeering, pointing, to you it's all a game
But you don't know her story, or even just her name.

They sit together alone, like they always do,
They're terrorists you say, they have put bombs in our food.
Once again you laugh tearing pages from the Quaran,
But you don't see them hurting, how badly your words caused harm.

How about the one with the darker pigment to their skin?
It should not be about looks, but the mind that lies within.
All the racist comments, they don't belong so they must go,
But honestly if they ever did leave you wouldn't even know.

You were too busy putting on a show, being rude just for the fame,
You forgot that colours, cultures, religions aren't the same
You can't blame a Muslim for what only some have done,
They really aren't the same there are more beliefs than one.
The same way you can't blame one black man, for other black men's sins
You should not base your first impression on the colour of their skin.

Tell me in life how far will you get,
If you can't treat people with equal respect?

Jemeya Molindo (14)
St Peter's CE (A) School, Exeter

Nobody Cares

Nobody cares about the children crying, the babies dying,
the people left alone in the world.

Refugees are leaving, asylum seekers seeking,
nobody cares for peace.

Terrorists are bombing, people are sobbing,
nobody respects them.

Religions are falling, ISIS comes a-calling,
nobody blames us.

The media paints a picture, war becomes a fixture,
everyone ignores the truth.

Society is falling, darkness comes a-crawling,
nobody cares about them.

Nobody cares that police are discriminating, no one is investigating,
we need to take a stand.

Everyone is hiding, the whole world crying,
nobody wants to fight.

Justice is failing, good works are trailing,
nobody is trying to help.

Society is falling, darkness comes a-crawling,
nobody cares about them.

Nobody cares about the teens self-harming, the children arming
themselves against the world.

Teen pregnancies are higher, now children play with fire,
nobody cares for safety.

No one here looks perfect, people no longer worth it,
nobody fits the bill.

That two-faced friend will judge you, no one longer loves you,
nobody's feelings are real.

Depression levels rising, kids are a-climbing,
everyone watches them jump.

Society is falling, darkness comes a-crawling,
nobody cares about them.

When the world trembles, every nation fumbles,
so nobody remembers them.

Hannah Quinn (15)
St Peter's CE (A) School, Exeter

Institutionalised

I've been institutionalised, statements filled with lies,
A failure in my family's eyes,
So hard to turn my life around when my hands are tied,
Stuck in a box while time passes by
Look up to the sky, begging for forgiveness,
Just to remember, it's only business

Always making the wrong decision, blame my unfocused vision,
Mind so frustrated, life so sophisticated,
How can I think outside when I'm stuck in a box,
With chains, keys and locks, trying to rebuild my life with these building blocks,
Surrounded by these four walls,
Endless phone calls,
Is it worth being at school?

Four people involved and I get the blame,
Consequences weren't the same,
I don't do this for the glamour or the fame,
But still every teacher knows my name,
Not for the right reasons,
Making it look like I've committed treason,

Can't you see what I'm stressing,
I can't learn from your lessons,
it's no longer myself I'm impressing,

Adrenaline rushing through my veins,
Reading textbooks just ain't the same,
Rules you're enforcing are nothing but stupid
Resulting in young kids getting excluded
You take my friends from me,
And tell me I was one to mislead them
One day, you wait, I will get my freedom.

Samuel L Vile (14)
St Peter's CE (A) School, Exeter

So This Is It

So this is it
the start of a new generation
of immigration-hating, power-loving citizens of the world
is this the way we want our children's lives to unfurl?

So this is it
Donald Trump has won
he's won the minds and the respect of only very few
divided opinions with his ideas whether they be false or true

So this is it
the end of an era
just as things were looking up, equality for all
Trump comes rushing in dividing nations, 'Let's build a wall'

So this is it
a new America
full of judgemental, hypocritical, brainwashed supporters
of a man who has no respect for reporters

So this is it
the people have spoken
we want freedom, division, independence and security
well the biggest threat America faces, is in charge of the country

So this is it
is this the end?

Or is it an opportunity for us all to make a stand?
For everyone religion, age, sex, and race, why can't we understand?

So this is it
I will say for the final time
I want you to think about what really matters in life
is it the colour of your skin, or where you were born?
Because I think what really matters is equality for all.

Jessica Yates (15)
St Peter's CE (A) School, Exeter

Earned By Default

'Respect your elders, they know more than you,
Think how they survived throughout World War Two,
They have great knowledge, their views are correct,
Think how they voted this president elect.'

Respect should be earned, we all get taught that,
But what about that anti-democrat,
He thinks he is big, his country is great,
With all the racism and women hate.

'Respect your elders, it's the thing to do,
It doesn't matter if they respect you,
Do as you are told, they know what's best,
They don't want to know what's on your chest.'

Respect should be earned, there's no other way,
But the youth are passed by day after day,
We ask for a chance, just to prove to you,
That we can do anything you can do.

'Respect your elders, do not answer back,
You know they're allowed to give you a smack,
They know their values, do not make them change,
Your generation is just very strange.'

Respect should be earned, there's no exception,
Don't accept someone's lies or deception,
Our generation, they say we don't fit,
But the ones that complain forget who raised it.

Mimi Mugford (15)
St Peter's CE (A) School, Exeter

Hallelujah Money!

Living off borrowed time, the clock ticks faster.
That'll be the hour we pay the tax masters.
Parliament snickering with sick laughter,
Come to cut branches on the verge of disaster.

The royals are sitting atop their throne.
While we're shovelling money into their home.
The middle man's tired, he's become violent-prone.
Greedy MPs are reaping what he's sown.

Meanwhile our healthcare is failing.
On top of that our national budget is caving.
Our old way of life is slowly decaying.
Society thrown in the wind and fading.

People are starting to give up the fight.
What poet has been libertarian right?
A perfectly planned plundering plight.
Hospitals are having to turn off their lights.

I-C-E cold, nice to be old.
Deficit increases from twice to threefold.
Selling bonds, lo and behold.
Bailing out the biggest crisis ever told.

It's precious, treat it like it's honey.
For people it's the only way to be sunny.
The situation's a mess, it's almost funny.
Blessed be tender, hallelujah money!

Joseph McLaughlin (15)
St Peter's CE (A) School, Exeter

There Are Easier Ways...

They send us to war
Away to die
We don't know what for
There's no real reason why

'Away to die!'
They said we should fight
There's no real reason why
Who's wrong and who's right?

They said we should fight
'Let's take over their land'
Who's wrong and who's right?
So much blood on our hands

'Let's take over their land'
It sounds pointless to me
So much blood on our hands
No one's really happy

It sounds pointless to me
Everyone loses
No one's really happy
All got black and blue bruises

Everyone loses
Our loved ones dead
All got black and blue bruises
or they die in their heads

Our loved ones dead
All fighting for peace
They die in their heads
But the violence won't cease

We're fighting for peace
But there are easier ways
The violence won't cease
Unless we change things today.

Maddie Arnold (15)
St Peter's CE (A) School, Exeter

Humans With A Heart

Black, white or any shade,
Skin colour shouldn't matter.
The Holocaust with its deadly camps,
Segregated schools, buses and toilets.
Racism drives society apart
But we're all humans with a heart.

Christian, Muslim, Buddhist, Sikh,
No faith's right, no faith's wrong.
Come together in peace, not violence!
Would any god want a war?
Religion can drive the world apart
But we're all humans with a heart.

Men labelled 'strong', women 'weak'
Everyone can be anything
The right to vote - women died for,
Every girl in education is still a dream.
Sexism drives genders apart
But we're all humans with a heart.

Whether you love men, women or both,
Love is what should matter the most.
For simply loving the same sex as you,
You face fear, judgement and punishment.
Prejudice drives people apart,
But we're all just humans with a heart.

Izzie Auty-Dawe (15)
St Peter's CE (A) School, Exeter

In The Eyes Of The Law

My mind is a jail to which I am chained,
And the day-mares and nightmares leave my body maimed,
My mouth is fixed shut and my eyes are inert,
My nurse is too loud and my doctor's just curt.

I don't want to live and I know that I'm dying,
But in the eyes of the law I have to keep trying,
I'm tired and lonely and with no words to speak,
Minutes to hours and days become weeks.

I want to give up but there's no chance I'm allowed,
'We'll never give up,' my son-in-law vowed,
Yet they're oblivious to my tear-streaked cheeks,
And my prayers for a death that have gone on for weeks.

Take me off this life support tech,
The money's a waste, I'm clearly a wreck,
One bottle of meds, would end all my pain,
And enable my family to breathe again.

I know it's hard for them to let go,
But I'm praying for an end, surely they know.

Eleanor Olivia Kerr (15)
St Peter's CE (A) School, Exeter

Perfection Is Overrated

Stop this labelling, stop this hatred
Let's say 'Perfection is Overrated'
You might not like what I have to say
But the truth is harsh, so face it anyway.

Why do you do this? Why to me?
Can you not actually see?
How much I try to be like you
It's harder for me but I'll get there soon

You're unhealthy if you're skinny
You're unhealthy if you're fat
You're gross if you're in-between
How messed up is that?

If you're blonde-haired, you're a bimbo
If you're ginger, you're stuck up
No matter what you're born with
We're all just out of luck.

Strength and willpower will silence the voices
This shaming shall finally stop
Pushing myself to make the right choices
In this battle, I'll come out on top.

Freya Fanson (15)
St Peter's CE (A) School, Exeter

I Want To Go To School

I want to go to school
But I can't, I can't escape
The never-ending cycle of back-breaking work,
Which traps me every day.

I want to go to school
But I can only dream. My parents will never send me.
Not when they gave me to these despicable men.
To grow tobacco for the rich people.

I want to go to school.
For what can I learn out in the fields,
The sweltering heat burning my neck as I work the hard, scorched ground?
Nothing. Nothing I tell you!

I want to go to school,
Where I can shed my chains, and aspire to achieve my ambitions.
They say I'm not a slave - they call me a child labourer.
But I know the truth.

And I don't like it...

Josh Nicholas (15)
St Peter's CE (A) School, Exeter

What Is Equality?

What is equality?
Equal in looks, equal in love, equal in loss
Is it treating someone with the same respect
That you would expect with no cost?

Are we really using our gifts,
To benefit others?
Our individuality to conquer?
Our talents to achieve?
If we're being sectioned into categories,
How is this to be believed?

Marching forwards and onwards,
He states to make it great,
To build up the wall
That generations recall,
Was knocked down by a switch of humanity.

I saw a little boy once,
Maybe nine or ten
But no matter the age
The opinions that were made
Were more promising,
Than the leader who towered above him.

Like a wall
A barrier.

The greatest thrive off others.
The weakest isolate with no
Courage.

Isobel Pinsky (15)
St Peter's CE (A) School, Exeter

Racism

I have been bullied many times before,
Each time saddening me more and more.
Just a single look at my face,
And they begin to judge me by my race.

Names and insults, I've heard them all,
Making me feel helpless and small.
Feeling as if I'm all alone,
Separated and on my own.

I have feelings too you know,
Broken, shattered, they will heal slow.
I have done nothing to you, so leave me be,
You're tearing me apart, can't you see?

I don't understand, why are you doing this to me?
We are all human, we should be treated equally.
Just because I am of a different race,
Does not mean that I am a disgrace.

Asher Condon-Jones (15)
St Peter's CE (A) School, Exeter

The Forgotten Land

The barren land stood limply
The buildings were like hands
Hanging like overgrown weeds
Over the forgotten land.

The trees had collapsed
None were left to stand
A pollution cloud through shade
Over the forgotten land.

The rolling fields were flooded
The explosion broke the dam
Perhaps someone wanted to rule
Over the forgotten land.

Graves were dug deep
Few could understand
Who could want to destroy
The forgotten land.

The explosion hit hard
By those whose hearts were cold
Now the forgotten land is a mystery
Never to be solved
Every inch a story
Never to be told.

Ellen Billingsley (13)
St Peter's CE (A) School, Exeter

Take Care Of The Environment

Take care of the environment
We've only got one
It's disappearing fast
An empty bleak landscape

We've only got one
It won't last forever
An empty, bleak landscape
Fight to get it back

It won't last forever
No trees, no fields and nothing left
Fight to get it back
It's in your control

No trees, no fields and nothing left
It's disappearing fast
It's in your control
Take care of the environment.

Anna Vukusic (15)
St Peter's CE (A) School, Exeter

Us, You, Me

Us, you, me.
Racism affects us all,
Through the news or through life.
It is wrong,
But aren't we supposed to be right?

Us, you, me.
Discrimination affects us all,
Through gender, age or choices.
Not everyone's the same,
Are we any better than the past?

Us, you, me.
We're supposed to be equal,
We're supposed to have free will,
We're supposed to be ourselves,
is life really how we see it?

Tristan Bentall (15)
St Peter's CE (A) School, Exeter

Ripples

As the ripples on
The grey pond
Disperse
So too
Does your memory

As my second,
Failed stone
Sinks,
So too does your
Spark

And as its
Ripples
Disperse,
So too
Does your memory

And the cycle
Begins anew.

Rufus Stanier (14)
St Peter's CE (A) School, Exeter

Behind A Lie

I was once heartbroken and alone
Having basically nobody to comfort me
So I wore a mask that always smiled
To hide my true feelings behind a lie.

Before long I had many friends;
Luckily with my mask I was just like them.
Although deep inside I still felt worthless
Like I was missing a part of me.

Nobody could hear my crying at night
For I designed my mask to hide the lies.

Nobody could see the pain I was feeling
For I designed my mask to show I was laughing.

Behind all the smiles would be tears
And behind all the comfort came all my fears.

Soon I realised my mask was worthless,
I only wore it because I was jealous.
My friends would notice something different
They told me that I was very 'ignorant'.

I didn't listen to them, not even once
I came across very blunt,
But soon I realised it was time to let go
Of the mask I used so nobody could know.

Bracken Kerr (12)
Stoke Damerel Community College, Plymouth

My School Rhyme

Life is tough
That's what they say
But they don't know
What it's like every day
To wake up in the morning
And go to school
So that people can test you
To see that you're a fool.

The teachers say
That you obviously didn't try
But they don't know
You go to your room and cry.

You did put in effort
You did your part
They just don't understand
That you're not that smart.

Then comes the pressure
From your mum and dad
Who are so clearly disappointed
That your grades are bad.

You are punished
And picked on
For the rest of the year

Because you finally gave up
On your future career
That was once so close
But now so distant
However your teachers
And parents
Are still insistent.

Jasmine Wilkins (12)
Stoke Damerel Community College, Plymouth

Nan's Poem

Nan, you were always the best,
Sweet dreams now you are at rest,
I love you more than words can say,
And miss you more and more each day.

I remember the times when we used to play together,
And I'll hold these memories forever and ever,
Although I can't see you, I know you're not far,
At night I'll look up at the sky as you are the brightest star.

Although we are apart,
There is always a place for you in my heart,
I will cherish the time we shared,
Remembering your kind words and the way you always cared.

I never got to say goodbye,
But I sent a prayer to you up high,
You will always be our beautiful queen,
With the greatest smile that's ever been seen,
It's sad but God only takes the best,
Goodbye, sweet dreams now you are at rest.

Bethany Hawkey (12)
Stoke Damerel Community College, Plymouth

A Nanny Like You

A nanny like you everyone should have
A nanny like you has eyes like nature
Not everyone has a nanny like you.

Your heart was as pure as gold
Her hands were like a key to a different dimension
You put grand into grandparents
Your eyes are like pools of water that went too far to look into
Because I would be too scared that I would never stop.

Your care would take me down memory lane
A nanny is a little bit parent
A little bit teacher
And all your best friend.

The tears that ran from your crystal-ball eyes
Were like gems falling from the sky
You will be the root of the family
And will always be the root of the family.

You were the wisest one of all of us
You were like the dictionary everyone would want
I love you Nanny.

Khloe Lyndon (13)
Stoke Damerel Community College, Plymouth

Date

She was eight, she was out late
She bounced a ball homewards before her in the last of the light
She'd been warn
She'd been told
It grew cold.

She took a shortcut through the churchyard
She was a small child making her way home
She was brave
She fell into an open grave.

It was deep, it was damp, it smelled strange
'Help!' she cried. 'Help, it's me!'
She shouted her own name out.

Nobody came,
The church bells tolled sadly; shame, shame.

She froze, she had a blue nose
She clapped her hands, she stamped her feet
In soft slip-away soil
She hugged herself
Her breath was a ghost floating up from the grave
Then she prayed.

She... was... late!

Alexandra Maticiuc (12)
Stoke Damerel Community College, Plymouth

Winter

The cold crisp air bites the end of my nose,
And the trickling snowflakes freeze my toes,
Walking up and down the frosty path,
Hearing robins chirping sounds like they can laugh,
Whilst walking to school,
We were throwing snowballs thinking we were cool.

We left tracks beneath the snow,
Thinking how cold it is, oh I know,
My ears were almost frozen off,
It was so cold I was trying not to cough.

Hot chocolate with extra marshmallows,
Whilst building a snowman, what an 'odd fellow',
My hands were freezing,
My friends were sneezing,
I couldn't wait to get home in the warm,
After the big winter storm.

Lucy Chugg (11)
Stoke Damerel Community College, Plymouth

Music And Me

Music in my head
Morning, noon and night
I love music so very much
It fills me with delight.

I put on my headphones
And play all my songs
I could listen to music
All day long.

Listening to music puts me a good mood,
It makes me want to stand up and groove.
Music is love or whatever it can be
Music's the life that's inside of me.

I will always want to sing for singing means so much.
It tells a loving story because it means so much.

My music will be with me until the day I die.

Sam Rickard (12)
Stoke Damerel Community College, Plymouth

There's A Monster In The Corridor!

I'm not lying, this isn't fake!
I was walking in the corridor,
When the lights went out,
Then I heard a growl and a great big bang!
I turned around,
There was nothing there,
So I began to run.
All the doors were locked,
Then I saw those big, red, bulging eyes
So I ran the other way
I'm not lying, this isn't fake!
There's a monster in the corridor,
Just go there at night
And you will see the awful sight!

Alana Hallybone (12)
Stoke Damerel Community College, Plymouth

Stop Bullying

Why do you do it?
Is it because you think it makes you hard?
Stronger?
Popular?
Why did you do it?

It hurts you know
We cry,
We cut,
We cry more
It hurts you know.

Why we cut
It's because of you
All you
because of what you do
Why we cut.

Stop!
Stop!!
Stop!!!
Why do you bully?

Joe Maddick (14)
Stoke Damerel Community College, Plymouth

Lauren Martin

L ove everyone
A mazing at art
U nderstanding and kind
R eally good at singing
E nergetic and fun
N ever tells lies

M y mum and dad are cool
A rms open wide, cuddle time
R eally caring person
T ime for fun with friends
I gnite that warm heart
N ow or never.

Lauren Ann Martin (11)
Stoke Damerel Community College, Plymouth

The Football And Its Friend!

The football is like your friend,
Whose friendship will never end,
The other team is like your enemy
Who like to give us penalties.

We spin and turn and pass the ball,
Along the muddy floor,
Whilst our shoelaces are untied
Because of all the running,
The team is cheering us on and...
Bam! Another goal!

Katelyn Bell (12)
Stoke Damerel Community College, Plymouth

Family

Family is the best thing in life,
But it can be trouble and strife.

Family is the best you can get,
But you can get stuck like fish in a net.

Family is the best present ever,
But if you can't accept that, you'll be alone forever.

Bradley Burgess (13)
Stoke Damerel Community College, Plymouth

Dance

If I could be something
I would be a dance:
Dance shows emotion
Dance makes you feel emotion
Dance is like a person but a better side
Dance is love in a creative way
Dance will make you smile or cry
Whatever day you may have had.

Klaudia Zawadzka (11)
Stoke Damerel Community College, Plymouth

Rollerskating

Saturday nights are our skate nights.
We skate till late
with our wheels on the ground,
spinning and skidding
till we fall down.
When the music plays
we bob along
to all of our favourite songs.

Cody Coombe (11)
Stoke Damerel Community College, Plymouth

Anxiety

Scared, angry, drunk with fatigue,
Living with the fear of failure,
Falling
Without any urge to be productive.

It's wanting desperately,
To be by myself,
Throughout each day gone and wasted,
Yet not wanted to be lonely.

Caring about everything,
Being passionate,
About the paradise world I live in,
Still, I don't care about anything.

It's wanting to talk to you,
To be able to speak up,
Loud,
But hating the idea of socialising.

I'm free,
I can run wild,
I can do anything and everything,
Yet I'm trapped within myself.

Soon I feel everything at once,
Bubble up inside me,
Ready to burst,
All at once,

Still I feel everything at once,
Still I care,
Still I want to be alone,
But soon I feel nothing at all.

Thea Scott
The Kings Of Wessex Academy, Cheddar

Animal Rights

Animals have rights
And just because they can't put up fights,
We think we can kill them right there and then,
What did that little fly do to offend?

You're more likely to be struck by lightning,
Than be attacked by a shark quite frightening,
Good thing that the wolf has its boys by its side,
if it didn't it would not survive.

From ants in yo' pants
To the great elephants,
I just want to live in harmony,
With our endless animal family.

Dylan Skinner (12)
The Park Community School, Barnstaple

We're All Equal

We're all equal, we're all the same
Why do us ladies have to go through the pain?
1901 is when the suffragettes took action
Emily Davison gave her life for our rights on Derby Day
Yet us women still didn't get a say.

We're all equal, we're all the same
Why do us ladies have to go through the pain?
For years we fought for what was rightfully ours
1928 the men gave in, finally women had won!
Without their fight our rights would be none...

Lily Wilson (12)
The Park Community School, Barnstaple

Discrimination

Equal rights;
Black and white.
If you are white and he is black,
Don't go away - don't turn your back!
You are equal to all that you see.
It has no price. It has no fee.
Your freedom and rights are all at your feet
So show respect to all that you meet.
Do not be harsh, shout or scream
Because everyone has a right to a dream!
Whether it is full of hope or temptation:
Don't let it cause the world's discrimination!

Phoebe Clarke (11)
The Park Community School, Barnstaple

Racism No More

Racism is all around,
Even in your local town,
Just because they're black and you're not,
Doesn't mean you can criticise a lot.
They're no different to all of us,
So stop saying they had to get off the bus,
Racism is not in you,
Segregation and discrimination too.
They have the rights to be in this world.
Black or white, we're all the same,
So stop giving them the blame.
This must stop. *Now!*

Lexus Jayne Dryden (12)
The Park Community School, Barnstaple

Mary's Abuse

Mary had a husband who,
Hit her when he liked to.
She cried and cried every night,
Until her room was bathed in light.
Mary did not tell a soul,
Because her husband would take his toll.
She hoped her husband would just stop,
But she was wrong; he did not.
Then he pushed her down the stairs,
She was dead, but he didn't care.
The image of Mary stuck in his head,
Because she was dead.

Lucy Camp (12)
The Park Community School, Barnstaple

Horse Abuse

Why do you do it?
Is there a reason for it?
What is the joy of putting them in cages
And leaving them there for ages?

Taking their life for fun
Don't pick up that gun!
Mistreating our favourite horse
Once a galloper around a sand course

You whip and whip until they squeal
Why did you do that dodgy deal?
We are against horse abuse
The fatal overuse.

Madison Fishleigh (11)
The Park Community School, Barnstaple

Poaching Is Wrong

Poaching animals is wrong,
When you point that spear so long!
You might think it's all fun and games,
When they die out, you're to blame.
If you're doing it for money,
Trust me, it's not funny.
If you use their head as an award,
By killing them with your disgusting sword.
If we find you in the wild
Your punishment won't be mild.

Poppy Tallin (11)
The Park Community School, Barnstaple

Deforestation Destructs

One tree down,
An animal's home destroyed,
More trees gone,
I am getting annoyed!

Extinction's coming around,
But you don't care
You're destroying trees
And it's going everywhere!

Ten species dead,
Half the jungle's gone
What is this life,
Oh please, you know this is wrong!

Lucie May Sandwell (11)
The Park Community School, Barnstaple

Equality

Everybody is born equal,
No matter the race or gender.
But sometimes people forget this fact
And make their own prejudicial agendas.
Even in the modern day,
Society still thinks it's okay
And with the rise of discriminating propaganda,
The public starts to believe that equality isn't the answer.

Ben Robinson (11)
The Park Community School, Barnstaple

Hard Life

I see their faces through the bars,
Mud slops around their feet.
Their eyes hold no expression;
Scarcely do they eat.
The poached ground where they stand
Bathes in the thick brown mush.
The overweight pigs sit around
Living their life so lush!

Rosie Anderson-Retter (12)
The Park Community School, Barnstaple

YOUNG WRITERS INFORMATION

We hope you have enjoyed reading this book – and that you will continue to in the coming years.

If you're a young adult who enjoys reading and creative writing, or the parent of an enthusiastic poet or story writer, do visit our website **www.youngwriters.co.uk.** Here you will find free competitions, workshops and games, as well as recommended reads, a poetry glossary and our blog.

If you would like to order further copies of this book, or any of our other titles, then please give us a call or visit **www.youngwriters.co.uk.**

Young Writers
Remus House
Coltsfoot Drive
Peterborough
PE2 9BF
(01733) 890066
info@youngwriters.co.uk